NUBIAN BOOKSTORE
PRESENTS

WHEN I GROW UP I WANT TO OWN...

Volume 2

WRITTEN BY MARCUS DEWAN WILLIAMS
ILLUSTRATED BY HH-PAX

NUBIAN BOOKSTORE
PRESENTS
Also By Marcus Dewan Williams

**Nubian Bookstore Presents: When I Grow Up I Want To Own . . .
Volume II**

Published by
Marcus Dewan Williams
Nubian Bookstore

Nubian Bookstore
1540 Southlake Parkway
Suite 7A
Morrow, GA 30260

www.facebook.com/Nubian Bookstore

Library of Congress Control number: 2020925064
ISBN 978-0-578-8564-9-0
Audience: 3 & Up
10 9 8 7 6 5 4 3 2 1
1. Children 2. Picture Book 3. Easy Readers
First Printing

NUBIAN BOOKSTORE
PRESENTS
WHEN I GROW UP I WANT TO OWN...

This book is dedicated to

Patrick & Tiwanna Stubblefield
Ike & Flurette Williams
Chadwick & Valarie Clark
Olevia Williams
Earnestine Williams
Stacye Williams
Polk A. Williams III
Kendrick & Natasha Williams
Terrence & Pia Williams
Jamero & Fatina Hatter
Katherine Overton
Shahrazad Ali
Professor Griff & Sole
Darryel (White Folks) Woodson
Jocelyn Dotten
Zawadi & Stacey Allen
Bennie & Debra Toney
Keith Saunders
Selma Quinn
Essila Ringer
Nia Damali (Medu Bookstore)
Christa Cochran

A REAL ESTATE AGENT helps clients purchase and sell homes, buildings, or land. They help clients find properties that they like, set the price of the property, and give their clients advice to help close deals.

A **JEWELRY STORE OWNER** designs and sells jewelry to customers and is responsible for daily operations. She is knowledgeable about different types of gemstones like diamonds, metals like gold and silver, and types of jewelry such as rings, necklaces, and bracelets.

A Nail Salon Owner oversees the operations and finances of her shop. She is responsible for hiring and training nail technicians. The owner ensures that customers receive manicures and pedicures in a clean and healthy environment.

A Law Firm Partner is an attorney with at least six years of legal experience who makes decisions at a law firm. She represents clients that have civil or criminal cases. She must have good communication and research skills and must be deeply knowledgeable about the law.

A Bakery Owner oversees daily operations and knows how to bake a variety of desserts including cakes, pies, cookies, and pastries. The owner hires and manages staff, orders baking supplies, and ensures that equipment is working properly.

A Veterinarian makes sure that animals are healthy. She examines pets to diagnose problems, treats their wounds, and gives them medicine when they are sick. She can perform surgery and advise pet owners on how to care for their animals.

A Dog Walker gets paid to take other people's dogs for walks. She and her clients agree on a schedule and place to walk the dogs. She also feeds the dogs and gives them water.

A Hair Salon Owner is responsible for making sure that clients receive hair and beauty services including washing, styling, and coloring hair. She and her staff may also apply makeup and provide skincare treatments. The owner is responsible for business operations, ensuring that equipment and tools are working properly, and supervises staff.

A Perfume Store Owner is knowledgeable about fragrances and helps customers choose products that smell good. She is responsible for ensuring that the shop has popular perfumes and cologne in the store, manages inventory, and supervises sales staff.

A Website Designer creates the layout and look of web pages. She creates code, designs graphics, inserts video, and formats text. The designer makes sure that links work and the website stays updated with new information.

A Shoe Store Owner is responsible for maintaining inventory with the latest shoe styles. She hires and supervises staff and makes sure that they greet customers and assist them with selecting shoes. The owner oversees finances, returns, and exchanges.

A Home Decor Business Owner plans the layout and function of rooms in a home or business. She selects furniture, paint color, decorative items, and lighting. An Interior Designer knows how to read blueprints and must have knowledge about industry codes and regulations.

A Clothing Boutique Owner runs her own retail store. She makes sure that the inventory is on-trend and helps customers select clothing that fits their personal style. The owner trains and manages staff and oversees business finances.

A **Certified Public Accountant** is a licensed financial professional who helps clients prepare their income tax returns. She is a qualified professional who assists people with filing their income tax returns.

A House Cleaning Business Owner cleans houses to get rid of dust, dirt, and germs. She uses safe chemicals, tools, and machines like a broom, mop, and vacuum to make homes sparkle.

An Architect designs buildings and homes. She uses a computer to draw blueprints for clients. She estimates costs, plans a timeline, and determines if a location is in the right place for the structure to be built.

A **SPORTS FRANCHISE OWNER** hire's the team's general manager, coach, and other staff. She plays an important role in picking the right team members. She helps negotiate contracts and handles day to day operations.

AN ICE CREAM SHOP OWNER makes sure that the equipment is working to dispense ice cream. She chooses the flavors and toppings that are offered to customers, provides good customer service, and supervises employees.

A USED CAR DEALERSHIP OWNER buys and sells preowned vehicles to customers. She takes customers for a test drive, negotiates contracts, provides financing, warranties, and takes payments.

A COMPUTER REPAIR WOMAN fixes computers. She knows how to use the latest technology and helps clients solve computer problems. She installs software and repairs problems with the hardware.

A PET GROOMER takes care of dogs and cats to make sure they look good. The groomer combs their hair and clips their toenails. The groomer also bathes animals and treats them for bugs that might harm them.

AN EYE DOCTOR makes sure that your vision is healthy. She performs tests to see if you are nearsighted or farsighted. The eye doctor also prescribes glasses or contact lenses.

A DRY-CLEANING STORE OWNER cleans customer's clothes by using special chemicals to remove stains and odors. She operates machines to press clothing and does alterations like hemming or stitching.

A **BOOKSTORE OWNER** manages daily operations of the business. She makes sure that the books from authors are on the shelves and helps customers find and purchase the books that they want to read. The owner provides good customer service and manages the bookstore finances.

A PERSONAL FITNESS TRAINER helps customers with a workout and nutrition plan to have healthy bodies and reach their fitness goals. The trainer motivates their clients to workout, shows them how to do exercises correctly, demonstrates how to use equipment, and makes sure that they do not get injured.

A PHOTOGRAPHER takes professional pictures of people, places, objects, and events. A photographer is trained to capture the best images using cameras and lights in a studio.

A SPORTS MANAGEMENT AGENCY OWNER provides legal representation for professional atheletes. She also helps negotiate contracts for their clients.

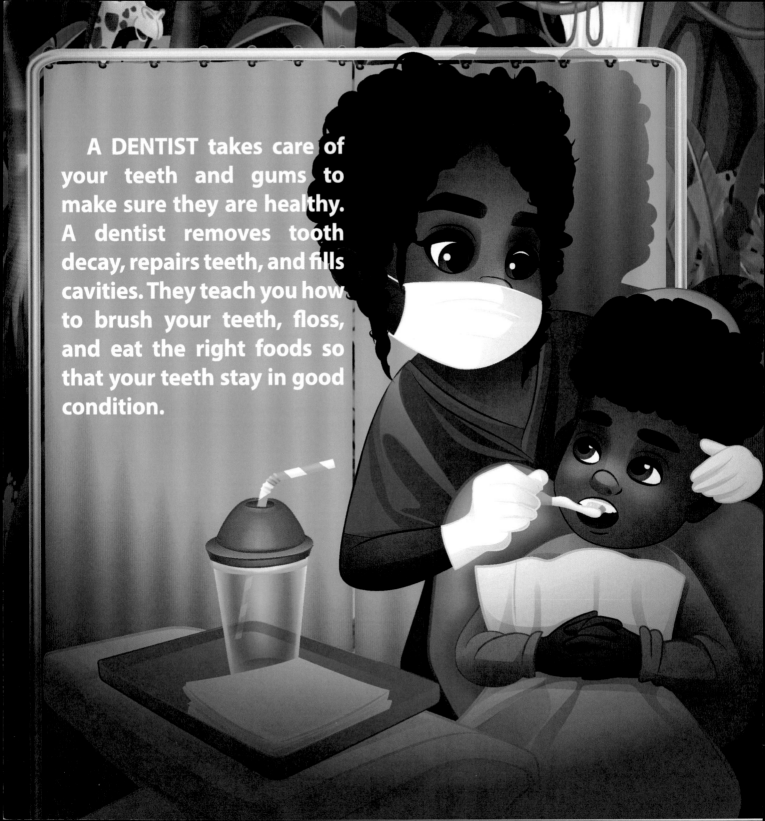

A **DENTIST** takes care of your teeth and gums to make sure they are healthy. A dentist removes tooth decay, repairs teeth, and fills cavities. They teach you how to brush your teeth, floss, and eat the right foods so that your teeth stay in good condition.

A MUSIC STUDIO OWNER is someone who owns a place where recording artists go to record their music. Music studio owners have all of the equipment needed to record music.

WHAT TYPE OF BUSINESS DO YOU WANT TO OWN WHEN YOU GROW UP?

REAL ESTATE AGENCY	SPORTS FRANCHISE	WEBSITE DESIGN
TAX PREPARATION	JEWELRY STORE	SHOE STORE
PET GROOMING	BOUTIQUE	ANIMAL CARE
HOUSE CLEANING	HOME DECOR	LAW FIRM
PHOTOGRAPHY	MUSIC STUDIO	NAIL SALON
ICE CREAM SHOP	PERSONAL FITNESS	EYE CARE
USED CAR DEALERSHIP	PERFUME STORE	DENTISTRY
BOOKSTORE	SPORTS MANAGEMENT AGENCY	DRY-CLEANING
ARCHITECTURE FIRM	DOG WALKING	COMPUTER REPAIR
HAIR SALON		BAKERY

YOU CAN OWN ANY BUSINESS YOU WANT!

NOTES

Made in the USA
Monee, IL
30 April 2022